Ichthyosaurus

Written by Ron Wilson
Illustrated by Doreen Edwards

Library of Congress Cataloging in Publication Data

Wilson, Ron, 1941-
  Ichthyosaurus.

  (The New dinosaur library)
  Summary: Introduces the ichthyosaur, or fish lizard, a reptile that swam like a fish, which first appeared during the Triassic period 250 million years ago.
    1. Ichthyosaurus—Juvenile literature.
[1. Ichthyosaurus.   2. Prehistoric animals]   I. Title.
II. Series.
QE862.I2W55   1984   567.9'3   84-11483
ISBN 0-86592-204-7

Rourke Enterprises, Inc.
Vero Beach, FL 32964

Diplodocus

Pteranodon

Woolly Mammoth

Ichthyosaurus

Allosaurus

Hypsilophodon

Ichthyosaurus

The young Ichthyosaurus was the smallest and weakest of the family. She had not received as much food as her brothers and sisters when she was an infant. She was still a weakling when the others were ready to leave their mother. As with all Ichthyosaurs, the young stayed with the female for several months. One by one, the others had gone their separate ways; only she remained. Only then, did she get all the attention and food that she needed.

Today something was not quite right. The mother Ichthyosaurus had become very restless. Her young offspring wasn't sure what the signs meant. She had never seen her mother like this before. The mother was driving the young one away from her.

Not realizing what her mother meant, she had returned repeatedly. Each time the mother became more agitated and drove the young one off.

The young Ichthyosaurus was confused. She wondered what the problem was. She stayed away. However, since she had never been left alone before, she kept her mother in sight.

As the young Ichthyosaurus swam around she noticed a large rocky outcrop. She moved toward it. As she did so she made many backward glances to ensure that her mother didn't disappear completely.

Unlike her brothers and sisters the young female had never engaged in the wild diving and swimming activities that they had. She had never had enough energy. Now somehow she managed to find enough strength to power her flipper-like paddles so that she could maneuver her way toward the jagged rock. The rock would provide suitable hiding places, and from its safety she could watch her mother's movements.

The rock was extremely large. She came closer to it. Crags hung out from it making the water around it very dark. Fear overcame her. She had never been on her own before. She made for a small overhanging ledge, disturbing a shoal of Pholidophorus. She sidled gently toward the ledge looking very carefully for other signs of life. It wasn't easy to see in the dim light.

The juvenile Ichthyosaurus suddenly felt something crash into her. A larger Ichthyosaurus had been using the same place for shelter. As the female moved back she crashed into another ledge.

Panicking, she left the safety of the rock. In the confusion she had lost sight of her mother. She didn't know what to do or where to go.

Then she spotted the dull outline of an adult Ichthyosaurus in the distance. She wasn't sure whether it was her mother. Slowly she moved toward the outline. It became clearer. She recognized the familiar figure. By now the young female was so relieved that she had forgotten her mother's earlier reactions. As she approached her mother, she was driven off again. This time, her mother was angrier than before. She lashed out with her large flipper-like paddles, missing the young creature by inches.

The young Ichthyosaurus was more than puzzled by this latest outburst. She circled around for a few minutes. She wasn't certain what to do now. She had never left her mother before — not even to catch her own food.

She continued to swim around cautiously. Each time another creature came by she backed away. Most were smaller than she was, but she had not really been taught how to fend for herself.

Short of air the young female made her way
slowly to the surface to fill her lungs. She had never
done this before on her own. Now instinct told her she
must do it. She moved upward.

One thing she had learned from her mother was
that danger often lurked above the water. It took her a
few minutes to reach the top. She paused just under the
surface for a few minutes. She looked upward.

Cautiously she poked her long snout out of the
water. She looked around. She was very close to the
shore. Looking up she could see the outlines of
Pterodactyls. As she watched, several of them left their
perches on the cliffs above her and dived toward the
sea.

Fear overcame the young Ichthyosaurus. For a few seconds she remained motionless, her head poking above the water.

Then she realized that the Pterodactyls were coming toward her. They had spotted a shoal of fish. She did not realize this; she thought they were coming for her.

She quickly gulped as much air as she could and withdrew below the surface. As she looked up she could see the form of the Pterodactyls flying toward the water.

The Ichthyosaurus dived quickly to a lower level. On her way down she passed her mother coming up. She slowed down as the two approached. Her mother ignored her and continued toward the surface. The young Ichthyosaurus turned for a moment so that she could follow her mother's upward movement. She paused, started to follow, and then decided against it. Instead she circled slowly waiting for her mother's return. She did not have to wait long. The large form of an Ichthyosaurus appeared. Keeping her distance the young creature followed in the older creature's wake.

The jagged rock appeared in the distance. The older female made for it. The young one followed. There was plenty of room for both of them to shelter.

As she neared the rock the young Ichthyosaurus could see clouds of mud rising. She paused for a moment, unsure of what was happening. Suddenly the form of a much larger Ichthyosaurus came toward her at great speed. It was very angry and left behind a trail of blood. She dived to one side and followed its movements. As she gazed at the fleeing creature it turned around and came back toward her. The trail of blood grew wider. Again she moved away.

The angry, injured Ichthyosaurus continued on its way toward the rock. More mud flew up. The young creature was curious. Carefully, she made her way to the rock. Two male Ichthyosaurs were locked in combat. A young female watched them. Eventually, the wounded male was driven off. The victorious creature turned to the waiting female.

The cloudy water was beginning to settle and the unattached female peered into the distance. She could now make out the outline of the rock.

She swam slowly around it, carefully looking into every nook and cranny. She had never really surveyed it before. It was massive and there were numerous hiding places.

The young Ichthyosaurus's survey took her a long while. She was very careful. She came to one overhanging ledge. She caught sight of a large tail fin. She hid behind an outcrop and studied it. She could see the rest of the creature. She recognized the form — it was her mother.

Her first instinct was to go toward her. She
didn't. She looked on rather bewildered at her mother's
actions. Then she caught sight of what she thought was
the form of a small Ichthyosaurus. Her mother had
given birth to her next offspring.

Now the juvenile Ichthyosaurus knew that she
was on her own. She turned around quickly, as
something prodded her gently. There, swimming close
by, was another young Ichthyosaurus. The newcomer
swam away and then came back toward her. She
realized it was a young male.

The moment had really come for her to break
her ties with her mother. It was now time to mate and
start her own family. She moved off, turning frequently
to glance at the young Ichthyosaurus watched over by
the older female.

Interesting facts about . . .
Ichthyosaurus

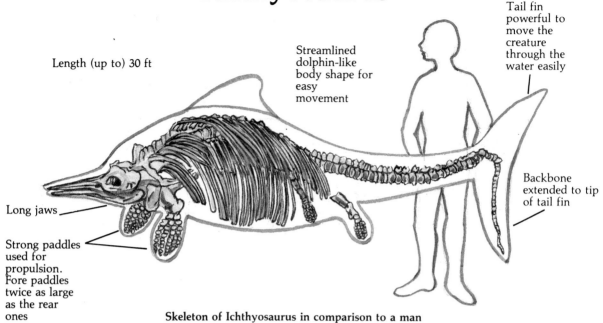

Length (up to) 30 ft

Streamlined dolphin-like body shape for easy movement

Tail fin powerful to move the creature through the water easily

Backbone extended to tip of tail fin

Long jaws

Strong paddles used for propulsion. Fore paddles twice as large as the rear ones

Skeleton of Ichthyosaurus in comparison to a man

What were Ichthyosaurs?

The Ichthyosaurs are known as "fish lizards". They first appeared in the Triassic seas 250 million years ago. So far scientists have not been able to discover where they came from.

The first fish lizard to appear was one called Mixosaurus. It is possible that this particular species developed from reptiles which lived on land. No one is certain. Why a land animal should change its way of life is a mystery.

There were other Ichthyosaurs living in the Triassic period, including one called Cymbospondylus. Ichthyosaurus did not appear until millions of years later in the Jurassic period (195 million years ago to 145 million years ago).

In between the true land animals and the true water animals were other creatures. It is likely that these were like modern amphibians — frogs and toads. Amphibian means "double life". Amphibians have to spend some of their life in the water if they are to survive. By Triassic times the first Ichthyosaur lived completely in the water.

The First Ichthyosaur Remains

The first Ichthyosaur remains were discovered in England at the end of the nineteenth century. A lady named Mary Anning found the first complete Ichthyosaur skeleton. Even before this, some vertebrae (backbones) had been found in 1712. The person who discovered them did not know to what creature they belonged.

Living in Water

Ichthyosaurs were called fish lizards because they had evolved from reptiles, but could swim like fish. Ichthyosaurs were able to move easily through the water because they were streamlined. They also had limbs like large paddles. These helped them swim well. Although all four limbs were paddle-like, the front two were twice as big as the back two. In general shape the Ichthyosaurus was like a dolphin. Some Ichthyosaurs were quite small. There were some 40 inches long. Others were much longer. The longest was about 40 feet in length. Ichthyosaurs had very powerful tail fins which they used to help them move forward. There was also a triangular fin in the middle of the back.

The creature's head was also streamlined. It tapered into a long thin snout similar to a dolphin's.

Preserved Ichthyosaurs

Some complete Ichthyosaur skeletons were found at Holzamaden in Germany. They were so well preserved that scientists could see the outlines of skin in addition to the remains of bones. From these remains scientists were able to see exactly what the paddles and fins were like. These Ichthyosaurs had been so well preserved, the color of the skin could be seen. The remains were in such good condition because when the creatures died they sank to the bottom of the sea. Here they were covered with mud. They were found many millions of years later.

What Did The Ichthyosaurs Eat?

We know what Ichthyosaurs ate because fossil droppings, called coprolites, have been found. These contained the preserved remains of the Ichthyosaurs' food. Some fossil droppings were found near Ichthyosaurs. Others were still inside the bodies of the dead creatures.

Inside the droppings were the remains of a fish called Pholidophorus. These creatures were believed to live close to the surface of the prehistoric seas. From their shape it is also thought that they were fast swimming creatures. Since Pholidophorus were fast swimming fish, Ichthyosaurus must have actively hunted their food. They caught most of it close to the surface of the water.

Other Ichthyosaurs fed on cephalopods. These prehistoric creatures were related to the octopi which live in today's seas. Remains of the cephalopods were found inside the dead Ichthyosaurs. The soft parts of these creatures had been digested. This left large numbers of small, curved, black hooks. These came from the tentacles of the cephalopods.

In the stomach of one young Ichthyosaur 478,000 hooks were found. This juvenile Ichthyosaur was only 60 inches long. It is calculated that this particular creature had eaten about 1,600 cephalopods. Living in the Jurassic seas at the same time as Ichthyosaurus were Plesiosaurs and Pliosaurs. Because all three kinds of marine creature fed on different food, there was no competition.

Things to do

Make models of the creatures in this story. You could use modelling clay. Instead you might like to cut out models from cardboard.

Look at one of the pictures in the book. Cut out the front from a cardboard box. Cover the inside with white paper. Paint a picture on this. Make model rocks from wire and paper mache. Color these. Cut out the shapes of some of the creatures in the story. Hang them from cotton so that they look as if they are swimming in your box.

You could make a puppet theater using a cardboard box. Draw, cut out and color cardboard creatures. You could then act out the story in this book.

Look through other reference books. Try and find modern creatures which look like Ichthyosaurus. See if you can find out what they eat. Look for pictures of squids and octopi. See if you can find out what they eat. You might also be able to discover what sea creatures eat squids and octopi.

Ichthyosaurs were similiar in shape to dolphins. See how much you can discover about these creatures.

The illustrations show three creatures which shared the same seas. They fed on different creatures so they did not compete for food.

Ichthyosaurus

Cryptocleidus
(Plesiosaur)

Liopleurodon
(Pliosaur)